Praise for
The Entrepreneurial Personality Type

The best information I have ever seen for entrepreneurs.

**— Russell Brunson,
founder of ClickFunnels &
author of *Expert Secrets***

Honestly, it blew me away. This information is mind-blowing. This is that big hug telling you everything is okay.

**— Dr. Kellyann Petrucci, M.S. N.D.,
author of *The Bone Broth Diet*,
host of the PBS specials,
*21 Days to a Slimmer,
Younger You and The 10-Day
Belly Slimdown***

The Entrepreneurial Personality Type is a game changer for all entrepreneurs and is a must-read. If you have ever felt alone or misunderstood as an entrepreneur, this book is for you. We are evolutionary hunters and we will not be denied! Thank you, Alex Charfen.

— Maya McNulty

No one "gets it" like Charfen. All I can think of is the millions of entrepreneurs who MUST get this information in their hands, brains, and daily lives! Reading this is not only like taking a breath of fresh air, loosening a vise grip, and placing a key piece in a complex puzzle. It's like a lifesaver for those on the rugged, lonely, solo journey that's full of noise and pressure for the EPT. Finally, someone who celebrates the glorious nuances of the Entrepreneurial Personality Type! Thank you, Alex Charfen! Thank you!

— Lisa Saladino Garife

Awesome guidelines on entrepreneurial strengths and how to leverage them into world-class results and avoid overwhelm, perceiving momentum as a key state of being to drive ultimate results was one of the most powerful things to change my life and allows me to jump in and out of momentum at will whenever I want. When I am in momentum, I feel like I'm operating 100x faster than everyone around me. Thank you, Alex, for your superb work in bringing this level of awareness, and connecting entrepreneurs from all over the world through the Entrepreneurial Personality Type.

**— Bruno Domingues,
founder and Managing Director
of Multiuniversal**

The book is short and to the point. Excellent.

**— Andrea Hutto,
Partner J. Austin Coin and Jewelry**

This book unleashed me. All my life I've viewed myself as a wannabe entrepreneur. My back trail is littered with failed projects, so at some point I decided that I wasn't a real entrepreneur. Negative feedback from the people around me, who did not understand EPTs, only reinforced my limiting belief. Despite the pain, I could not help myself, after a sometimes too long phase of selling my soul to the devil, I'd step up and reach for the brass ring again. After reading Alex's book, I now know beyond a shadow of a doubt that I'm not broken, there's nothing wrong with me. I'm just different. But the best type of different. If you suspect you're an EPT, or love one, get this book. It will profoundly shift how you see and understand the world!

— Brad Codd

It is almost as if Alex wrote *The Entrepreneurial Personality Type* about me. Never have I seen a book that has identified who I am and that it's okay to be this way. As Alex said in the book, "Entrepreneurs are always called crazy until they start making money. Then they're brilliant." Awesome book.

— Andrew Miller

In a world where we are labeled for our passions and convictions because we are "different," thank you for reminding me that our issues are our strengths. This book truly has become my business bible.

— Anna Selby,
founder of Venture REI

The most important book I have ever read.

— Nancy Klensch,
founder and CEO of Summit Kids

Your book is incredible. I keep referring back to it in my decision-making process. After I read your book, I quit my job in Maine, which was holding me down and full of negative stimuli, and I'm now in Belize starting my new venture with all the right people. Such a GREAT read for any EPT who needs a little clarity about themselves and their abilities.

— Gary T. Lovett,
Retired USMC

Superb—100% inspiration and a huge contribution.

— Brian Kurtz,
founder of Titans Marketing LLC and
author of *The Advertising Solution*

Ever feel like you were born to change the world but felt weird saying it out loud? This book will speak to you in ways few others can. I've always felt different, but not because I'm in a wheelchair. It's because I felt "wired" to do big things, and I never understood why... until I read this.

— Jon Morrow,
CEO of Smart Blogger

My whole life, I've always felt like there was "a better way" of doing everything I encountered. Not necessarily my way but a better way, and I could never do things as if there wasn't. This often led to problems. I alienated people, jumped from job to job, and often felt like I was walking a line between a great discovery and simple arrogance. *EPT* is the validation I wish I'd had when I was younger to know that what I have is a gift, not a challenge. And I get to benefit from it every single day.

**— Ari Meisel,
author of *The Art of Less Doing***

I quote Alex Charfen more than any other expert. He has truly decoded the mind of an entrepreneur. Learn everything you can from this man.

**— Sean Stephenson,
professional speaker and author
of *Get Off Your "But":
How to End Self-Sabotage
and Stand Up for Yourself***

Alex Charfen, I love you, man. You've done more for my growth and headspace than anyone I know. Your writings—*EPT*, the blogs, the vlogs, the podcasts—have been revolutionary to me, my wife, our relationship, our business, and our life. Following your basics, we have 4x'd our business and are currently working on moving completely away from brick and mortar to virtual service. I cannot thank you enough for your guidance and wisdom. Every entrepreneur, from the beginner to the "know-it-all," needs to read this book and listen to your words. Again, in one word...REVOLUTIONARY. Thank you.

— Jason Bradley

The first time I read this book, it gave me goosebumps. The things he talks about... it's like he was calling to my soul. The second time I read this book, it made me cry. Another layer peeled. Another revelation. Another moment of total understanding. The third time I read this book, it changed me forever. Something unleashed and broke free. Suddenly instead of trying to fit in and be normal, I realized I didn't want to fit in. I didn't want to run with the crowd and, better yet, I wasn't even made to. Alex's words helped me to understand myself in a way I didn't know I needed and gave me answers to questions I didn't know I had! I'm an EPT and I'm damn proud of it. I am forever grateful to Alex for writing this book and making it available to every misunderstood, hurting, bound, or buried EPT out there. Thank you, Alex. You are one of the greatest mentors I will ever have.

— Marley Baird,
CEO of Marley Baird Media

If you are looking for something that can easily change your life, then look no further. Alex has been an extremely successful entrepreneur for decades and has worked with probably more CEOs than any other person I have ever met. Consume each page while taking notes. To me, this book is the entrepreneur's bible!

— Gallant Dill,
CEO of GallantDill.com

As a business owner, the feeling I have always craved the most is being in momentum. This book, along with Alex's work, has been a game changer. It explained so many weird things about my personality and made me realize that even though I am a weirdo, I'm in very good company. If you want to get your momentum back, or just make sure you're in momentum every day, read this book now. You'll be glad you did.

**— Taki Moore,
author of *Million Dollar Coach***

The *EPT* book opened my mind. I'm not alone…and I'm not crazy. I'm an EPT! I've followed so many entrepreneurs. Charfen is one of the few who we stop, drop, and follow. His advice is spot on in *EPT*. The pressure and noise as an EPT is, at times, crippling. Charfen's guidance has unlocked my mind and prepped me and my team for the next level of success…and beyond!

— Rachael Pederson, founder of Social Media United, The Viral Touch

I've always known I was different, I just didn't know there were so many other people like me. *The Entrepreneurial Personality Type* let me know that I am not alone.

**— Steve Sims,
CEO of Bluefish**

I first got a copy of the *EPT* book at the Titan Summit where Alex and I were speaking. I read the book in one night and immediately had context for my life. I understood why certain things were working for me and why others weren't. Most importantly, that I was not crazy and that I was not alone. The book and Alex have helped me on my entrepreneurial journey, and I'm infinitely grateful.

— Greg Wells,
CEO of The Wells Group
and author of *The Ripple Effect*

This book is a must-read for any visionary entrepreneur that wants to change the world.

— Giovanni Marsico,
founder of Archangel

The Entrepreneurial Personality Type was incredibly instrumental in my overall purpose and vision for moving forward as an entrepreneur. Never before have I seen a message with such intention and meaning around who we are as entrepreneurs and constant creators of momentum. If you are an entrepreneur, you feel the pull of being a momentum-based personality type who drives forward and wants to change the world in huge ways. As entrepreneurs, we need more help than most other occupations, but we also feel that any request for the help we need makes us feel exposed and weak. This book helped me understand in a profound way that not only is there nothing wrong with me (as society often makes us feel), but also that I am not alone when it comes to getting help with the mission and vision I try to create daily. Alex's messages is that when we understand ourselves better and stop our limiting behaviors, we can create unlimited momentum. You owe it to yourself to learn what other industry leaders and billionaires have leveraged from EPT to reach incredible levels of self-understanding and peak performance.

**— Jarrod Warren,
J. Warren Consulting Systems,
Inc. and The Success 101 podcast**

I'm on my fifth reading. If you are even thinking of becoming an entrepreneur, drop everything and read this book.

—Edward Tang,
CMO and Co-founder of MoooFit Ltd.

My life and my family will never be the same.

—Edward Elliott,
Husband, Father and Lifetime EPT

EPT is a game changer! It should be required reading for entrepreneurs and evolutionary hunters everywhere!

—Laura Slinn,
Co-Founder of Avalon Empowerment
and Author of *Conscious Conception*

I've never understood myself better until reading the EPT.

—Matt Ogle

This book should be mandatory reading
before starting any entrepreneurial journey.

**—Dave Lindenbaum,
Founder of Make Cool Stuff LLC**

I've been in the publishing industry for a long
time and I rarely hear something completely
new. Alex Charfen's *Entrepreneurial Personality
Type* was exactly that a groundbreaking and
life changing discovery. I am eternally grateful
because I feel like it explained me to myself
for the very first time.

**—Dennis Welch,
President of Articulāte PR
and Communications**

The Entrepreneurial Personality Type

Your Guide To The Most Important And
Misunderstood People Among Us

By

Alex Charfen

Note: Entrepreneurial Personality Type and its initialism EPT are registered trademarks. However, the ® symbol has been omitted from most mentions in this book so as not to distract from the content.

Print ISBN: 978-1-944602-30-7

Thanet House Publishing
848 N. Rainbow Blvd. #750
Las Vegas, NV 89107

Publisher's Cataloging-In-Publication Data
(Prepared by The Donohue Group, Inc.)

Names: Charfen, Alex, author.

Title: The entrepreneurial personality type : your guide to the most important and misunderstood people among us / Alex Charfen.

Description: Las Vegas, NV : Thanet House Publishing, [2019]

Identifiers: ISBN 9781944602307 (print) |
        ISBN 9781944602314 (ebook)

Subjects: LCSH: Businesspeople--Psychology. |
Entrepreneurship--Psychological aspects. | Success in business--Psychological aspects. | Creative ability in business.

Classification: LCC HB615 .C43 (print) | LCC HB615 (ebook) |
DDC 658.421019--dc23

Cover Design by Eled Cernik
Interior Layout by Soumi Goswami
Illustrations by Karina Arnal

To Cadey, Reagan, and Kennedy, Gustavo, Jeanie, Michelle, Melissa, Vanessa, and everyone like me who has struggled to find their place in the world

Contents

Preface

The Hunters

The evolution of entrepreneurial behaviors

Years ago, the tribe knew them as the Hunters.

The tribe loved the Hunters. They knew the truth: Hunters were essential for survival. Yes, they were different, but their differences were what made them great. Those differences made them willing to do what no one else would, and to accomplish exactly what the tribe needed to survive.

The Hunter was one of us.

You know those people, right? Can't sit still, motor always running, would kill a wooly mammoth and barely get it back to the cave before thinking about the next adventure.

They wake up energized every day, sharpen their weapons, and then go out to meet the sun and whatever peril the day may bring.

I know this because I've always been a Hunter. From as early as I can remember, I have gotten up before the sun, biologically compelled to track prey or the opportunities and challenges ahead.

I started in the business world when I was eight years old, working for my dad. As an awkward kid who was isolated and bullied at school, I found much-needed solace and acceptance in the sales conversations and transactional nature of business. I understood the marketplace far better than the classroom. Even then, I sensed that business was what changed the world for the better, and I knew I wanted in.

It quickly became clear that I had no choice. Business and commerce chose me. And I'm glad it did, because it probably saved my life. I found comfort in commerce and built my life around business. Through the years, I have made a fortune...and lost it all. Then I made another fortune, and this time I figured out how to protect it and build upon it.

Now I'm no savant. I've made big mistakes. But I've been right a lot too.

My prey wasn't just business opportunity and sales, but also knowledge. I've read thousands of books and studied every great Hunter from Plato to Benjamin Franklin to J. K. Rowling. I'm constantly consuming data and information and discovering new Hunters, more people like us.

Society tells us how different and unique we all are as humans. But Hunters are much more alike than they are different. While incorrigible, impatient, frustrating, and confusing, they have all been relentless in their pursuit of what's next. More than 10,000 tries to invent the light bulb? A completely natural pursuit for Thomas Edison, Master Hunter. Build a car that redefines possibility on four wheels, while simultaneously developing a space exploration company? Not a problem for Master Hunter Elon Musk. Even Bill Gates, famed for his (achieved) goal to put a computer in every home, has channeled his energy toward enhancing lives around the world, including the elimination of AIDS, tuberculosis, and malaria in the developing world. Having developed the Gates Foundation into the largest transparently operated private foundation in the world, do we really think he can't do it?

The list of Hunters and their great accomplishments is endless, and their drive to contribute to the world has no limit.

Still, the strengths that make Hunters so successful also make them "crazy." But that is society's way of making sense of them. How else can we explain Virgin's Sir Richard Branson, IKEA's Ingvar Kamprad, and Azul Brazilian Airlines' David Neeleman all being diagnosed with attention deficit hyperactivity disorder (ADHD), and yet becoming captains of their respective industries? Henry Ford and Steve Jobs were diagnosed with dyslexia. How did this not stop them from literally changing the world? Pablo Picasso suffered from bouts of deep depression. Was this necessary to create some of the most transformative (and valuable) works of art the world has ever seen? Society needs such labels to understand the ways in which Hunters don't conform to established standards for behavior.

I suspect that all of the late and great legendary Hunters throughout the ages would now be labeled with some kind of identifier that supposedly helps the rest of the world understand them better: troublemaker, disciplinary problem, workaholic, manic, bipolar, ADHD, compulsive, obsessive, hyperactive, anxious, disordered, or even disabled. The problem is that these labels in and of themselves can create enough pressure and noise to cause the symptoms they describe. They become self-fulfilling prophecies.

Many of today's star Hunters were not eager students in the traditional sense. Some use their keen drive to gain an advantage to "game the system" and succeed. Others are highly sensitive or future-focused visionaries who appear constantly distracted. Schools were set up for compliance, and Hunters just can't comply. They are always thinking about how to do things better, and that doesn't sit well in an organization clinging to tradition and standardization. Hunters resist and avoid this kind of constraint because they know they can do better, and nothing will stop them from trying.

I tried, and I spent most of my school years wandering the hallways or sitting in the principal's office. Rarely was I rewarded for being a Hunter in school.

Too many of our young Hunters today find themselves confined to an educational system where the goal is sitting still, memorizing equations, and taking multiday standardized tests. Those who fail to comply—because they simply can't—find their natural strengths and attributes suppressed. Unable to forge their own paths, the most sensitive and demonstrative Hunters are rejected, attacked, and backed into a corner, forced to react as any Hunter would. The proof is in our overflowing juvenile detention facilities and the young adults crowding into our prison facilities.

It's the nagging question "How do I get ahead?" that compels us to gain some sort of advantage in the world. Without guidance, protection, and support, this question drives some of us to break the law. I wonder where these people would have been if they had only recognized their so-called issues as strengths. Could seeing themselves as leaders and not outcasts have saved them?

Growing up, I struggled. I stood in the shadows a lot, tried not to be noticed, and barely scraped by in school. And sometimes I didn't know if I would make it. I finally found success, because I realized that what made me different could be used to build something amazing.

The Hunter is hardwired to contribute and support the tribe. Evolution has physiologically conditioned Hunters to care, because without others, nothing they do matters. Around the world, we see creative works, charitable foundations, endowments, and public institutions set up as monuments to great Hunters who shared their fortunes with the tribe, our world. Today, our tribe knows the Hunter by another name: entrepreneur.

Society calls them the 1%. It thinks they made their money fast and easy. They seem to leave one successful company to start the next, just because they can. Everything comes easy to them, right?

The historical argument that the wealthy create human suffering must be updated and corrected. Entrepreneur isn't a dirty word. These Hunters are creating wealth in unprecedented amounts and in previously impossible timeframes. Through Facebook, Mark Zuckerberg has connected people all over the world and helped facilitate social revolution. Hunter Jessica Alba, unable to stop her compulsion to contribute, transitioned her focus from the silver screen to establish The Honest Company, helping families live toxin-free.

The Hunter is a momentum-based being, seeking and thriving on the sensation of moving forward, and believing the impossible is possible. As the masses desperately cling to the status quo, Hunters press on in search of innovation and contribution, the same way our species seeks oxygen after being held underwater.

And so, to all you Hunters who feel broken in some way because of an itch you can never scratch, because you constantly dream about the next adventure, because you look out the window and swear you can see what could happen if everything went perfectly...

Sharpen your weapons, rally your teams, and set your course, because here's some welcome news...

There is nothing wrong with you, and you are not alone.

Changing How We See
The World

*Our instinctual focus on deficits over
attributes*

When I talk to groups of entrepreneurs,
I often begin by talking about the Hunter
and the tribe, because that's where everything starts for us—the good and the bad.
Our entire society has emerged and evolved
from those early tribes. They're why we
stick together, share responsibilities, look to
improve each other's lives, and create order.

The tribe was formed to increase humanity's
likelihood of survival against almost impossible odds: harsh weather, wild beasts, and
other hostile tribes. And we did survive, in

spite of our weak and unprotected bodies and relatively slow running speeds.

The tribe was foundational to our survival. So were the lessons it taught our ancestors. Primary among these lessons was to identify each other's deficits.

Focusing on deficits made perfect sense. Within our tribe, it could mean the difference between life and death, between the tribe's survival and its ultimate demise. As Hunters, we needed to know who was blind or deaf, who had only one eye, one arm, or one leg, because they would limit our ability to provide for and protect the tribe. For this reason, tracing back to our earliest ancestors, we have been evolutionarily conditioned to see deficiency as a threat to survival.

Today, we live in a time when our environment can make up for any of our shortcomings. We have evolved past the need to link deficiencies with survival.

Unfortunately, our instincts have not.

Despite overwhelming evidence—the blind man with incredible hearing, the deaf woman who is highly attuned to body language, the dyslexic student with powerful memorization skills—society is too accustomed to seeing the world in terms of deficits and exceptions. And so are we.

In trying to improve, we naturally default to identifying and focusing on our weaknesses—our supposed deficiencies—in hopes that we can become better by figuring them out. Millions of books, courses, self-help seminars, gadgets, and apps have been created to "level up" our weaknesses. Even case studies have been written to evangelize the benefits of these tactics. But beware, because there's an inherent danger in focusing on your deficiencies. And don't just take my word for it.

Oprah Winfrey, a towering entrepreneur for the ages, once said: "What you focus on expands, and when you focus on the goodness in your life, you create more of it."

So what are we doing by focusing on our deficits? We're creating more of them. We're enhancing them. We're actively expanding the power of our deficits to limit our capabilities.

To embrace and realize your entrepreneurial potential, you must choose to see the world and yourself differently. See opportunities in the exceptions rather than limits. See the attributes that must be enhanced rather than deficiencies that must be fixed. This is what makes people exceptional. This is what unlocks the limitless possibilities set out before you.

The change is easy, but it must be intentional. Every action—including things such as exercise, planning, proper hydration, sleep habits, and decision-making—should intentionally amplify your attributes. In this frame of mind, no challenge is too difficult, and no constraint can hold you back. Negativity will roll off your shoulders, issues will seem less intense, and you will find yourself effortlessly propelled through your day.

Once I started looking at the world this way, I couldn't turn it off. Entrepreneurial attributes were everywhere, marking every step, decision, invention, and innovation. So I decided to look further. I read hundreds of books and studied history. I interviewed a number of experts from psychologists and professors to start-up founders and serial entrepreneurs with 40 years of experience.

Then something strange happened: what I focused on began to expand, and I started to see the same attributes repeating themselves in the success of others. Great philosophers such as Aristotle and Socrates; revolutionary thinkers such as Andrew Carnegie and Madam C. J. Walker, an entrepreneur and philanthropist who rose from poverty to become one of the wealthiest African American women of her time; scientific geniuses like Marie Curie; innovators like Walt Disney, Sara Blakely (Spanx founder), and Warren Buffett; trendsetters like Coco Chanel and Sean "Puffy" Combs. It was everywhere, and it was so clear.

Generation after generation, successful entrepreneurs were not driven by random behaviors but by a core set of distinct attributes. Nowhere had I found these characteristics identified or listed as a coherent body of work. But in their entirety, they piece together something new, unique, and (until now) undiscovered: the Entrepreneurial Personality Type®.

Entrepreneurial Personality Type (EPT)

A consistently misunderstood subpopulation driving human evolution

The Entrepreneurial Personality Type (EPT) is a previously unidentified and misunderstood population that has lived among us for generations. Their personality type provides unique abilities. They see the world differently. They have particular sensitivities and are highly affected by constraint. But with the right support and guidance, they will contribute to humanity and change the world.

In short, the EPT is a meta-personality type identified by a cognitive and physiological response to momentum, or the sensation of moving forward. As such, the specific attributes of the EPT are highly sensitive to constraint, or anything limiting their momentum. When protected and supported, EPT attributes develop into unique skills and abilities, and often create unexpected outcomes. When suppressed, these same traits can be destructive or appear as disorders. For this reason, it is crucial for EPTs and their support systems (friends, families, managers, teachers, therapists, coaches, and others) to have a clear understanding of the attributes driving their behavior and perspectives.

The EPT is not a vision I have for the future or a reflection on what could be. It has been evident throughout history in the biographies, letters, and writings of famous leaders. As I take you through the attributes, you may begin to see evidence of their presence in yourself and others. You may find that they have been with you your entire life. You may feel a connection to something that seemed to be missing in your life. And you may even come to the realization that you have been suppressing these attributes for years, based on the negative interactions you've had with others. This is an unfortunate and all-too-common reality for EPTs today.

First and foremost, my hope in discovering and sharing the EPT is that it illuminates a singular message for every person who identifies with this type across the world...

There is nothing wrong with you, and you are not alone.

We Are Momentum-Based Beings

Our physiological attachment to momen-
tum and our sensitivity to constraint

Entrepreneurial Personality Types (EPTs) are momentum-based beings, meaning they have a mental, physical, and biological response to momentum, or the sensation of moving forward. As such, EPTs also have negative responses to constraint or anything hindering their ability to move forward. This affects their emotional states and their understanding of where they fit in the world.

When I talk to entrepreneurs about this concept, most of them instantly agree and realize it clarifies their behaviors and reactions to the world around them. But some remain confused by the terminology. This is understandable,

11

because for most of our lives we have thought of momentum purely from the perspective of high school physics. So what does that have to do with who we are and how we feel?

Perhaps one of these situations sounds familiar to you.

- You wanted to move forward but couldn't. Progress was slow and exhausting. Every step forward was chased by another step backward.

- You wanted to get unstuck but couldn't. Something was holding you back. You were overwhelmed and became your own biggest obstacle to moving forward.

- You wanted to achieve your goals faster but couldn't. You didn't know how or what was missing. The entire universe felt against you.

momentum

The good news is that we've all been there. You are not alone.

These situations and feelings are common, especially among EPTs, and they are the signposts of momentum-based beings. Feelings of frustration, stagnation, and constraint indicate that you are searching for momentum in your life. Understanding this will help you begin to clarify how you make decisions, how you react to challenges, and the reasons behind your behavior (good, bad, and neutral).

It may even illuminate the forces behind your emotional states. In fact, many momentum-based individuals identify with the sensations of forward movement and constraint more strongly than with traditionally labeled emotions.

Have you ever found yourself confused or alienated by cartoon "emotion charts" with faces that seem happy, sad, frustrated, and angry?

For you, these are just words, ultimately covering just three states of momentum.

How are you feeling today?

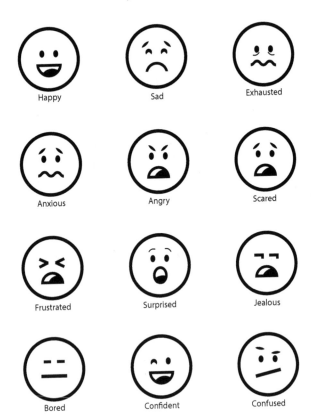

Moving Forward (fulfilled, elated)

Some refer to this state as Zen, flow, or even the feeling of being alive. In this state of momentum, we feel like we can accomplish anything, that nothing is out of reach, challenges are easy to overcome, and the path to success has been paved before us. This is the state in which we light the world on fire because we have removed constraint from our lives.

Moving Backward (frustrated, but challenged to push through)

When confronted with constraint or challenges, we can feel like we're moving backward, like our goals are moving further and further away from us. This feeling is highly frustrating. But while setbacks happen in life, they are often what prompt us to show up, bounce back, and overcome adversity. For momentum-based beings, this state can turn into a constructive period of realization and positive behavioral change.

Standing Still (wasting away, dying)

This is the most challenging state of all, because we often don't understand how to break free. Standing still, hitting a plateau, or being stuck makes us crazy. It drives us to drastically change our lives, make challenging decisions, and sometimes even harm our businesses or ourselves. We express this state cognitively by making poor decisions and feel it physically through stress and emerging body pains.

It is critical to understand that whether the momentum (or lack thereof) is real or perceived, the sensations and reactions in these states will be the same. It is a fundamental outlook that can cause EPTs to have challenges in environments of constraint such as rigid classroom structures, social relationships, or traditional business settings. It has also resulted in the systematic suppression of EPTs through negative reinforcement, behavioral change, and even medication, as their attributes and behaviors are often mistaken as disorders. It's a sad truth, but according to the National Alliance on Mental Illness, approximately 1 in 5 US adults (43.8 million or 18.5%)experiences mental illness in a given year. Well-marketed conditions like anxiety, ADHD, depression, and bipolar disorders are becoming so commonplace that diagnoses are growing at double-digit rates year after year.

For this reason, as momentum-based beings, it is imperative for EPTs to find ways to generate and sustain momentum in their lives.

EPTs have been misunderstood for far too long, rudderless in a world that provides misdirection and bad advice at almost every turn. In your journey to find and build momentum, you will need to understand yourself and the core group of attributes driving your behaviors. Focus on these and they will expand into great strengths and abilities, helping you generate momentum to make your greatest contribution to the world.

EPT Attributes

*The unique traits that create brilliance
and the symptoms of disorders*

The EPT is defined by a unique set of attributes that, when developed, transform into unique skills and abilities. Some EPTs even appear magical. We wonder how Steve Jobs created the most valuable company in the world. What was Albert Einstein thinking that led him to change the way we all look at the universe? Did Larry Page and Sergey Brin know that their upstart search platform at Google would become the way nearly everyone accesses online information? Throughout history, the EPT attributes have facilitated incredible, transformational achievements.

Following are some of the most significant characteristics of EPTs.

Attribute #1: High Sensitivity and Awareness

When it comes to high sensitivity and awareness, we must appreciate that our perception of light, sound, smell, taste, temperature, and mood can be different from that of our peers. Beyond a mere preference for certain types of foods, fragrances, or textures, an EPT's sensitivities can be heightened to the point of distraction. Some EPTs find it difficult to be around certain smells—especially chemically generated ones such as cologne or air fresheners—or to handle specific materials such as flannel, cotton, styrofoam, or other synthetics. Similarly, our heightened awareness can make us act strangely when we sense changes in environment and behavior. We've mostly learned how to suffer through these sensitivities and situations. However, when understood, embraced, and focused, they can become strengths and abilities that set us apart.

Each EPT has their own unique sensitivities and heightened awareness that can seem extrasensory. In speaking with thousands of EPTs, I've found some great examples: a conductor's perfect pitch, a marketer's awareness of social dynamics, a chef's unique taste pairings, a salesperson's ability to sense their client is dealing with a crisis.

Personally, I have some extreme sensitivities that help me connect visual content with audience perception. I'm regularly consulted to help refine video content before final production and to enhance broadcast opportunities before they go live. One time, when asked to give feedback on a friend's marketing video for a national ad campaign, I gave 44 revision suggestions—most of which were incorporated—although it had already been reviewed by several professional editors.

But it wasn't always this way.

Looking back, I realize these sensitivities were evident in my early childhood, in my reactions to light and the awareness of shadows. They were constantly on my mind. They drove me to be distracted in classrooms and uncomfortable in social situations. Fluorescent lighting would make my vision shaky and cause periodic blind spots. And as a kid being bullied at school (a nice way of saying "tortured"), I began to suffer from full-blown panic attacks because of them.

In changing our perception of heightened sensitivities and awareness from deficits to attributes, EPTs can develop them into strengths for achieving success in business and in life. It can be valuable to think through your particular sensitivities and consider how you might leverage them to your benefit. They could quickly turn into points of distinction and greater value.

Attributes In Action

Richard Branson, founder of the Virgin Group and its empire of successful businesses, does not hide his dyslexia. In fact, it's one of his more prominent distinctions as a global business leader. But many don't know that Branson was unable to fully understand his revenue statements until he was 50 years old, well after he had become a billionaire. His success did not come from simply working harder. Branson's dyslexia resulted in greater sensitivities to the simplicity of processes and heightened awareness of business trends, the dynamics of people and markets, and the core motivations of his customers.

Attribute #2: Future-Focused Outlook

The future-focused attribute often goes by another term: visionary. This label has become a badge of honor for successful EPTs. Struggling EPTs, however, get a different label: hopeless dreamer. The only true distinction between the two is how much protection and support the EPT has around them, helping to make their dreams a reality.

Put another way, dreaming is not unique. But it IS unique to have a vision, vividly imagine how it can happen, and then be compelled to make it a reality.

I say it often: entrepreneurs are always called crazy…until they start making money, then they're brilliant.

As EPTs find ways to enhance their future focus with the right teams, resources, and support systems, their "dreaming" will quickly transform into the brilliance of visionaries.

Attributes In Action

Steve Jobs, the legendary EPT behind Apple and Pixar (and also NeXT), had a persistent focus on the future, following his dream to change the world. He lived by the mantra "The people who are crazy enough to think they can change the world are the ones who do." In this case, "crazy" is simply how the present describes someone trying to make the future a reality. While this perspective often made Jobs difficult to deal with or work for, his future focus rallied teams, customers, partners, investors, markets—and eventually the entire world—around his vision.

Attribute #3: High Processing Capacity

An EPT's high processing capacity is often their most distinct differentiator in business. They can seem like machines, able to consume and retain information faster and in greater quantities than most others.

I often see this in EPTs who sound like experts in history, philosophy, physiology, engineering, or mechanics, despite their lack of formal training, even when they're among college professors and thought leaders in those fields.

In terms of behaviors, this particular attribute presents in two ways.

First, when looking to achieve a desired outcome, EPTs seek out and collect large amounts of data, regardless of physical or cognitive limitations such as deafness or dyslexia.

Second is an EPT's ability to process this information in order to cast a clear vision, take action, and make constructive decisions over time.

What differentiates EPTs from those simply able to read fast or memorize large amounts of information is that they are driven to analyze the data they consume and apply insights to achieve a result.

Attributes In Action

Beloved EPT Elon Musk was profiled on *60 Minutes* around the time he founded SpaceX. Interviewer Scott Pelley asked what qualified him to start and run a space exploration company, given that Musk had no history or training in the field. "I read a lot of books," Musk replied. As an EPT, his ability to consume data through books and apply the learnings allows him to realize his vision of SpaceX, as well as Tesla Motors…and SolarCity.

Attribute #4: Persistent Adaptability

EPTs maintain a persistent adaptability to take on new tasks or careers. No, they're not chameleons, able to adapt to any situation. In fact, many EPTs have difficulty adapting to certain situations like school structures or social environments. They may actually avoid or resist those situations.

In reality, this attribute is a persistent adaptability to new tasks and careers that helps EPTs achieve their vision or desired outcome.

This often leads EPTs through nontraditional (or multiple) career paths, where they gather diverse skills along the way.

Throughout my career, I've been a car cleaner, a payment processor, an executive recruiter, a technology sales consultant, and an on-air personality. Every step along the way was something new, but I was anchored by my desired outcome and future focus. I persistently adapted to different situations and the skills needed to address my challenges.

This is a story echoed among so many EPTs who often feel lost due to their varied professional histories. What's interesting is that the feeling of being lost is actually a reaction to the desire for a new outcome, not the frustration with constantly changing direction. It's helpful to look back at your various careers and jobs through the lens of progressive adaptation. As you adapted to each situation, you built and developed new skills, new perspectives, and new capabilities, all of which add up to enormous value for any organization you build.

Attributes In Action

As a boy, real estate mogul Dean Graziosi had a goal to become financially independent so he could take care of his mother. So when his family needed to increase their income by renovating a rental property, Graziosi quickly learned about electrical wiring, plumbing, and even operating a backhoe. Neighbors and contractors would stop by and ask his parents, "Who taught your son to do those things?" His father would admit that no one had, and Graziosi had figured it all out on his own. With a clear outcome setting his course, he persistently adapted to the skills necessary to move forward, all before he had even turned 13.

Attribute #5: Intense Focus on Results or a Single Outcome

There are myriad examples of EPTs being viewed as super- or subhuman in order to make their marks on the world. Oftentimes, they pulled back and isolated themselves (even the extroverts) in order to get things done. But the key to this attribute is that it centers around the pursuit of clear results or outcomes.

When not accompanied by success, this intense focus is rarely thought of as a positive attribute. In fact, when out of control, it can make EPTs appear obsessive, compulsive, combative, or antisocial. However, throughout history, this focus on results or outcomes has driven EPTs to change the world.

Attributes In Action

Robert De Niro is among the most famous and accomplished American actors today, having garnered two Academy Awards and seven total nominations. A lauded method actor, De Niro prepared for roles by immersing himself in his characters, their cultures, and their languages. He's perhaps most well-known for moving to Sicily to learn how to play a young Vito Corleone in Francis Ford Coppola's *The Godfather: Part II*. There, he not only learned

Italian but also perfected different Sicilian accents, much to the amazement of his voice coaches. De Niro knew the lengths to which he needed to isolate himself to fully focus on accomplishing his goals, and he was rewarded with an Academy Award for Best Supporting Actor.

Attribute #6: Bias for Improvement

As future-focused individuals, EPTs see the world not as it exists but as it should be. They see what should be modified, improved, or evolved. Given the choice between keeping things as they are or changing them for the better, they will almost always choose the latter. EPTs are innately driven to, and biased toward, improvement.

Without structure or support, pressure and noise can lead EPTs to question their improvements, which leads to more and more changes.

We see this kind of "improvement paralysis" in the architect whose designs are never quite done, the manager who's never ready to ship his product, and the writer whose manuscript collects dust on the bookshelf but is never submitted to a publisher.

When nurtured and mentored to see the fundamental principles for moving initiatives forward, EPTs can turn their visions for improvement into realities.

I've personally struggled to aim this attribute in a positive direction, finding myself in situations where my focus on improvement has become a constraint on my momentum. Perhaps you've been there too. Ultimately, I've found that reminding myself of the intended outcome allows me to set proper priorities and focus on the improvements that actually move me and my business forward.

Attributes In Action

Tim O'Brien has authored some of the most influential pieces of American literature, helping shape national policy and public recognition of the atrocities of the Vietnam War, and winning a National

Book Award for his novel *Going After Cacciato*. Despite the numerous recognitions and acclaim for his works, O'Brien still insists on editing his books each time they are reprinted. (He has nine novels with numerous reprints.) What some might call perfectionism, an EPT understands as a necessary bias toward improving what they put into the world.

Attribute #7: Experimental/Experiential Learning

Yes, EPTs learn through books and by consuming large amounts of data, but they truly seek the application of those learnings, the experiences and experiments; otherwise they don't feel momentum.

Many EPTs relate to this attribute in the context of sports, debate, contests, or other types of competition. These environments set clear outcomes and timeframes, forcing participants to try, learn, and adapt quickly. This is why we see the EPT attributes evident in so many professional athletes. Over the years, we've watched people like Roger Staubach, Michael Jordan, George Foreman, Shaquille O'Neal, and Steffi Graf make the transition from athletic success to great achievements outside of stadiums and arenas.

Unfortunately, as children, this attribute can make the traditional classroom and learning structures challenging for EPTs. When a greater focus is placed on memorization and standardized testing, EPTs lose interest or even skip established processes altogether to look for more practical applications.

Experiences and experiments give EPTs confidence to push further, validate what they've learned, and enhance belief in their visions of the future.

> **Attributes In Action**
>
> Fail fast; fail forward. Silicon Valley encapsulates this mantra, and no one better embodies this spirit than Mark Zuckerberg, who turned a college-dorm–specific registry site

(which would have struggled for any type of profitability) into the most powerful social network in the world. In the early days of Facebook, Zuckerberg held hackathons for talented developers to take on tough programming challenges, which amplified creativity and sped up innovation. As the company grew, these innovations turned into new offerings, platforms, and services rolled out to its users. Some worked; others failed horribly. These failures caused some early investors to call for Zuckerberg's removal as CEO, but he remained committed to experience and experiment with new applications from what he and his team had learned. As a result, Facebook became a highly profitable social platform with more than two billion daily active users and a stock price that has grown exponentially.

Attribute #8: Perception of Unique Connections

When the majority of people are united in one belief, it takes a certain type of person to offer contradictions or alternatives.

An EPT's ability to perceive unique connections in the world—through their experiences, experiments, focus on the future, and high sensitivities—brings different perspectives to any situation. They are able to see situations, problems, solutions, and processes from different angles in order to leverage new resources or move in new directions.

Sometimes this can appear to be divergent logic or the combination of conflicting ideas. However, an EPT's unique connections are driven by a focus on outcomes and the search for momentum, which provides context and guidance for these connections.

Especially in marketing, I've seen countless examples of EPTs making unique connections in their messages between audience interactions and the subtle shifts of language, color, positioning, or timing. As a sales consultant for Fortune 500 and Global 100 brands, it was my job to identify and execute on unique connections between products and the new markets and territories they sought to enter, and I was amazing at it.

Think about that. Big business pays a premium for access to an EPT's ability to perceive unique connections. They do this because they know unique connections can result in huge sales numbers and can spark trends, galvanize consumers, and move entire industries in new directions.

Attributes In Action

Brian Chesky and Joe Gebbia met as students at the Rhode Island School of Design and, in 2007, shared an apartment in San Francisco. Every year, San Francisco plays host to a number of high-profile industry events. However, in 2007, Brian and Joe perceived a unique connection between their unaffordable rent and the lack of hotel rooms available for the Industrial Designers Society of America conference. Purchasing three air mattresses, they marketed their idea and converted the first "Airbed and Breakfast" customers. Today, their company, Airbnb, has over 4 million lodging listings in 65,000 cities and 191 countries.

Attribute #9: Drive For Gained Advantage

An EPT's drive for gained advantage often begins with a single question: "How do I get ahead?" Do you remember asking this of yourself?

This question consistently drives EPTs through life to find an advantage or the means to get ahead. Most of us think of this as finding ways to increase income. This is valid and often our first motivation to understand business, finance, and people. But the drive for gained advantage can also mean escaping to a place that lowers pressure and noise. It could be the software developer retreating to a secluded room to code more effectively, the athlete putting in one more workout, or the realtor leveraging new marketing platforms.

In general, EPTs gravitate toward activities with a scoreboard (physical or perceived), a way for them to measure their advantage, because they are driven to win. The scoreboard also provides a frame of reference and validation for their momentum.

However, this attribute can turn EPTs into cutthroat individuals. As children, angling for a gained advantage can make it hard to collaborate with classmates or make close friends. However, it can also help EPTs of all ages understand not only how to turn their visions into reality but, upon starting a business, help them realize how to increase the contribution of their team members.

This is perhaps the most recognizable yet misunderstood EPT attribute. How many times have you heard yourself or other entrepreneurs talked about as being "only out for themselves" or "looking to win at all costs"? I'm not going to lie, I've heard this more than a few times about myself.

The truth is, the drive for gained advantage is a competitive attribute that enables EPTs to seek out new and unique solutions to shared challenges. While it is difficult to control how others react to this, EPTs have a responsibility to support and enable each other in their pursuit of these advantages. They are the foundation for how we move mountains. And by increasing awareness about how valuable this attribute can be, we can positively change the overall perception of EPTs.

Attributes In Action

Jeff Hays' drive for gained advantage has taken him across industries. He's achieved success doing everything from selling encyclopedias to broadcasting on local television to creating patents and finally establishing Capstone Entertainment, an award-winning film production company. Labeled a genius as a child, Hays always had supreme confidence in his abilities and would put himself first to get ahead, clinging to every advantage he could find. But after an awakening to the power of his ability to make a real difference and change minds, he began leveraging all his resources to produce movies that created movements and revealed hard truths. Hays has channeled his drive for gained advantage to lead himself down a path to change the world.

Attribute #10: Innate Motivation

Most EPTs can pinpoint the time in their lives when an innate motivation kicked in and they couldn't turn it off. For me, it was around age six (and my parents have confirmed it). For others, it can hit in their twenties or thirties. And for some EPTs, it happens even later as they approach retirement.

Typically, EPTs have no idea where this "fire" comes from. It appears suddenly and it transforms them. Their friends and family see a different person, someone capable of achieving anything.

Some view this attribute as mere ambition, but I'm not talking about a desire to climb corporate ladders or collect awards and recognition. Innate motivation is an engine with no off switch, a constant drive to accomplish tasks, achieve goals, and contribute to the world. All of a sudden, the EPT realizes there are more opportunities and possibilities to grow. There are standards that must be changed, expectations that must be reset.

Naturally, innate motivation can also make EPTs restless, impatient, and combative, especially around people who either lack the same kind of motivation or become obstacles to their momentum.

Attributes In Action

It's no secret that Bill Gates has become one of the most successful (and wealthiest) entrepreneurs in history. What many don't know is that his drive to succeed started at a very young age. As Gates was growing up, the potential for computers was only just being realized, so as a teen he would sneak into the computer lab of a local university to learn more about these fascinating machines. Beyond mere curiosity, his innate motivation compelled him to break rules, investigate, learn more, and enhance his skills, leading to the creation of a global technology juggernaut in Microsoft. But this success didn't satisfy his innate motivation. In his twenties, Gates continued his relentless pursuit of innovation, and he never took a day off in that 10-year span. Today, having given up leadership of Microsoft, his innate motivation has led him to establish the Gates Foundation, which has grown to become the largest transparently operated private foundation in the world.

The EPT Attributes Spectrum

The contradiction of entrepreneurial strengths

Most Entrepreneurial Personality Types share a similar feeling of being different or somehow set apart from their peers, and they have experienced it most of their lives. While the EPT attributes shed light on the source of those feelings, they're really only half the story.

Just as we EPTs see ourselves as different, unique, or exceptional, others can use labels like oddball, troublemaker, or unruly in describing us. This isn't necessarily because they're mean, but because EPTs are misunderstood.

Our EPT attributes drive our behavior and how we react to the world around us. When protected and supported, these characteristics can turn into strengths that make us appear magical. However, high levels of pressure and noise can make our traits show up as challenging behavior. I call this variation the EPT Attributes Spectrum, whereby particular EPT attributes can be enhanced or limited by varying degrees of pressure and noise. Table 1 provides a simplified breakdown of how these attributes can appear under different circumstances.

When EPTs better understand how significantly pressure and noise affect their unique strengths and abilities, they will seek out more beneficial environments and support structures. Similarly, when those surrounding EPTs recognize certain signs of high pressure and noise, they can better support EPTs and create those beneficial environments.

Strength under high pressure & noise	Attribute	Strength under low pressure & noise
Edgy, distracted, anxious	High sensitivity & awareness	Perceptive, intuitive
Hopeless dreamer, not present	Future focused	Visionary
Socially awkward, mind racing, indecisive	High processing capacity	Quick, accurate, machine-like
Constantly changing, haphazard, risky	Persistent adaptability	Capable, multitalented
Obsessive, antisocial	Intense focus on results or a single outcome	Determined, committed
Obsessive, compulsive	Bias for improvement	Constructive, creative
Slow learner, skeptical	Experimental/ experiential learner	Learn quickly and effectively
Cutthroat, antisocial	Drive for gained advantage	Looking for leverage
Activity without result, restless	Innate motivation	Go-getter, more productive than most

Entrepreneurial Suppression

How societal systems create unnecessary constraint for EPTs

With our constant search for momentum, and our existence across the EPT Attributes Spectrum, society is a tough place for EPTs.

As an organized structure of humans, society has inherent goals for behavioral conformity. This is typically a good thing; people generally know where to go, how to act, and what not to do. The system works really well when everyone plays by the same rules. And since rules are generally difficult to change, society is similarly resistant to change. So when there are people who can't or won't play by the rules, society has formed ways of dealing with them. I call this **entrepreneurial suppression**.

Figure 1 details how positive or negative stimuli can either enhance or suppress the natural attributes of EPTs.

For example, let's think about this in terms of the future-focused attribute. This manifests in the action or behavior of talking about the future, what's next, what could be. With positive stimuli (protection and support), EPTs become more aware of this behavior as a benefit, further developing this attribute and enhancing their ability to more concretely envision the future and make it a reality.

On the other hand, negative stimuli (discouragement, obstacles, pressure, and noise) will make EPTs see this behavior as undesirable. Just like burning a finger on a hot stove will stop someone from touching it again, the negative stimuli will naturally reduce the EPT's desire and ability to think about the future. Over time, the future-focused attribute will be suppressed and sometimes appear to be lost entirely.

It is important to note that the attribute will
only be enhanced or suppressed if the EPT
is aware of the positive or negative stimuli.
For example, if a person gives them feedback about an issue, the EPT may not realize
that they need to correct anything unless that
is overtly stated. Subtleties in communica-
tion are often lost. Without this awareness
or any concern for the development of the
attribute, EPTs will not progress in either
direction.

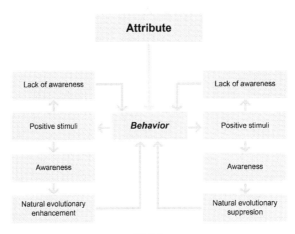

Figure 1

These conditions are seen throughout our society, and are especially evident in the increasingly rigid structures of our education system. This structure is a challenging place for EPTs to find success, and many self-select suppression in order to adapt to a world that does not entirely understand them. In fact, while there are instances where entrepreneurial suppression is a deliberate act of fear, jealousy, or dislike, the vast majority of suppression is due to an EPT's environment or circumstances, or simply a result of being misunderstood.

But there is one idea that all EPTs must know deep down in their hearts, to combat and push through the negative stimuli:

There is nothing wrong with you.

This simple awareness will help EPTs recognize perceived deficits as attributes and resist their systematic suppression.

Entrepreneurial Loops & Spirals

How loss of momentum drives
self-destructive patterns

"Insanity: doing the same thing
over and over again and expecting
different results."

— Albert Einstein

I love this definition, and it is never more true
than when applied to Entrepreneurial Personality Types.

If entrepreneurial suppression is the world's
way of burdening EPTs, then **entrepreneurial loops and spirals** are what EPTs do to
themselves. These loops and spirals illustrate
how, without proper intention, an EPT's

search for momentum and desire to take immediate action can turn into a destructive process that limits their ability to generate it. The first step in avoiding them—or breaking free from them—is to understand the hallmarks of an entrepreneurial loop (Figure 2).

The loop begins when an EPT perceives a loss of momentum, like static business metrics or confusion on how to move their career forward. As momentum-based beings with strong innate motivation, they then feel they must try and find a solution quickly. In this state of urgency, EPTs are often compelled to buy a solution, any solution, to help them get unstuck. This can be anything from a seminar to a book to a new technology platform for their entire business. But the perceived loss of momentum clouds our judgment and triggers us to take action without intention or a clear outcome in mind.

Interestingly, even just the decision to move forward or buy something will create a feeling of positive gain for EPTs. Then that feeling is enhanced by actually consuming the content or experience. While this feels like moving forward, remember that in an entrepreneurial loop, there is no clear outcome that EPTs are driving toward.

Instinctively, EPTs will sense that their feeling of momentum is false, and when they finally check on the progress they've made, they cannot verify any real forward movement. They can, however, verify that they have lost momentum again. If EPTs do not break out of this loop, and the process is allowed to continue, it will magnify in intensity and create a downward spiral of empty consumption and stagnation.

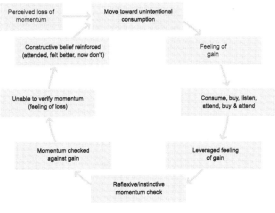

Figure 2

EPTs looking to break free from these negative loops and spirals (or avoid them altogether) must set goals and desired outcomes from the start, before ever deciding to attend an event or make a purchase. This ensures that their initial consumption of events or experiences will be intentional and measurable, and as they're able to measure, EPTs can understand what is actually providing them with momentum.

Perhaps you've seen some examples of this or remember a time when you were stuck in an entrepreneurial loop. Maybe Figure 3 is all too familiar to you.

Today, there are so many smart products to consume and inspiring opportunities for us to take advantage of. It can be easy to think that just purchasing one of these will get us unstuck.

I often see EPTs attending an excessive number of industry events and professional seminars, sometimes more than 30 in a year. I've also known some EPTs who listen to multiple podcasts every day, read two books a week, and join seven professional organizations, sustaining this consumption for more than a year.

None of these activities are inherently negative in and of themselves. However, to provide any value or generate the momentum an EPT is looking for, they must have that clear intention toward a desired outcome.

I actually believe these entrepreneurial loops have been with EPTs for generations, evolving along with humanity. Let's take a look at our ancestors, the Hunters, in Figure 4.

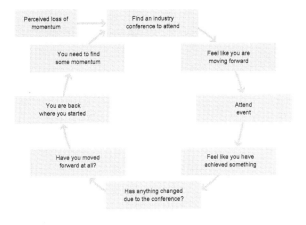

Figure 3

Following their need to provide for the tribe, a chemical reaction told their bodies to do something. So it was hunting time. Their bodies then told them this decision was a good thing, making sure they followed through. Heaven forbid it was in their nature to quit or forget about the hunt.

They hunted and they felt great about it. The Hunters were providing for the tribe, ensuring its survival.

But after a little while, they stopped and asked, "Did we kill anything? Do we have anything to give to the tribe?" They looked amongst themselves, turning their hands over and seeing nothing.

"No? Okay, it's hunting time again."

Luckily, the Hunters had a clear outcome. Their actions were intentional because their needs were simple. Today, EPTs don't have such a luxury. We see our objectives shift on a regular basis, and end up on multiple hunts headed in different directions. However, it's validating to know why we are so susceptible to these entrepreneurial loops. There is power in understanding that this is part of who we are, and our awareness will help us act with greater intention in finding real momentum in our lives.

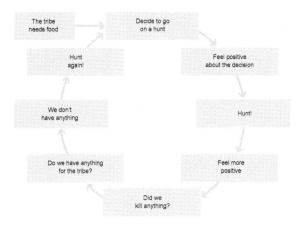

Figure 4

Mastering Overwhelm

Transitioning from constraint to confidence

While entrepreneurial loops and spirals are situational and based on a perceived loss of momentum, EPTs deal with challenges on a more regular basis. Our innate motivation drives us forward compulsively, and we have the tendency to take on big challenges, often more than one at a time. This is why EPTs often complain about being overwhelmed.

In breaking it down to its basic elements, I have found two key aspects contributing to overwhelm for EPTs. The first is an **unknown outcome**. Without a clear outcome in mind, all of your activities will be unintentional and you will lack the ability to achieve a meaningful goal. More to the point, you will not be able to generate momentum. Your disconnect from the sensation of moving forward leads to feelings of frustration, confusion, and helplessness, which touches upon the second aspect of overwhelm: pressure and noise.

The pressure and noise in your life act as constraints to moving forward and finding momentum. The pressure of deadlines, quotas, or financial needs can limit your ability to prioritize effectively. The noise of clutter, technology, and constant requests for your time can be highly distracting. Combine this with an unknown outcome, and you have the recipe for an overwhelmed EPT.

Math has a funny way of clarifying things for me, making numbers and situations feel more manageable somehow. So I've found that the simplicity of looking at these elements together in an equation can be insightful. This way, I can identify the sources of my overwhelm and, in the moment, move to correct them.

Unknown Outcome
+ Pressure & Noise

Overwhelm

But mastering overwhelm is not as easy as saying, "Know your outcome and eliminate pressure and noise." In fact, sometimes this is not even an option. Working in a large organization, you may not be in control of your ultimate outcome. And anything such as your work environment, relationships, injury, or illness could be sources of pressure and noise that are difficult to control.

Luckily for EPTs, there is a corresponding formula for us to combat overwhelm and gain momentum. This equation is all about finding clarity in the moment to gain confidence, and confidence trumps overwhelm any day of the week.

Clarify Today
+ Partially Clarify Outcome

Confidence

When EPTs are able to clarify today and stop looking at tomorrow or somewhere down the road, they can more easily understand what they must accomplish to move forward. Even the recognition of that task, that first step to take, generates momentum. It lowers whatever pressure and noise is coming from the future, which cannot be controlled, and helps to partially clarify an outcome. I say "partially clarify" because the main goal in mastering overwhelm is gaining confidence, and for that, all you need is a little bit of clarity.

In overwhelming situations, an inch of clarity can mean a mile of confidence.

An EPT's Fundamental Life Questions

The foundational path that guides EPTs to live in full contribution

You've learned about your connection as an Entrepreneurial Personality Type to our earliest ancestors, the Hunters. You've found a new way of expanding your contribution to the world by looking at strengths, not deficits. You've discovered the critical role of momentum in your life and the core attributes driving your behavior and perspectives. You've identified how society can constrain you, and how you can remove yourself from negative situations to continue moving forward.

As an EPT, you've entered into the most important and influential lineage in humanity, because you have the attributes, drive, and potential to change the world and actively evolve our society. The life of an EPT is an incredible journey, and even if you're nearing the end of your professional career, there is so much more you have to offer.

You see, most people live life wanting answers handed to them. They want the process figured out, the end goal clearly defined, and their paths brightly illuminated.

That's not good enough for EPTs.

EPTs live their lives confronting established norms and questioning the status quo. They welcome clarity but exist in the gray area of questions, where the search for a greater truth (their vision) creates momentum.

Whether you know it or not, your life has been playing out a series of questions that every great EPT has experienced and answered. Amadeus Mozart, Oprah Winfrey, Mary Kay, Nicolai Tesla, even JAY-Z—have all followed a predictable pattern of larger life questions throughout their lifetimes and careers. These questions illuminate a path toward acceptance, understanding, growth, and, most importantly, contribution.

Following are some of the questions that drive EPTs as they move through various transitions in their lives.

How do I stop pressure and noise?

Think back to the circumstances in your life when you were growing up. This was likely one of the first questions that arose. It may have been preverbal when you didn't have the ability to express how you were feeling.

Due to their attributes, EPTs deal with greater amounts of pressure and noise. It can be physical differences like slow development, learning differences like dyslexia, or social differences like trouble establishing relationships or discord at home, but they set us on a path to find ways of lowering pressure and noise in our lives, often at an early age.

What is wrong with me?

We ask this question our whole lives because we are different, and society's systems not only don't work for us, many of them work against us. We feel like there is something fundamentally wrong with us. In fact, since EPTs consume large amounts of information from books and seminars, the entire self-help industry is built around this question.

How do I get ahead?

This is often the first sign and recognition of our potential. Out of the question "What is wrong with me?" comes the question "How do I get ahead?" This is the first sign of the EPT's competitive nature and drive to be in momentum. We look for ways to make things better for us and learn what it takes to move forward. Our ability to disassociate from various aspects of our lives becomes profound.

How do I get further ahead?

To reassociate, we must often revisit some of these less positive aspects of our early lives and work through them in order to proceed successfully. This is possibly when our innate motivation kicks in, or when an influential person in our lives gets involved to amplify our efforts. You may need to find ways to "game the system" or simply try to survive… or both. This question is about leverage and typically leads EPTs to think about building a team for support. For any struggling entrepreneur, sometimes all it takes is encouragement and important people in their lives expressing belief in their abilities. This can change everything.

How does my team help me get ahead?

Here we start to see value in other people, but often in a self-serving way. EPTs stuck on getting further ahead can enter a selfish period of finding leverage through resources, especially people.

How do I help my team get ahead?

This is the transition that changes entrepreneurs' lives. EPTs quickly realize that the success of a leader is directly tied to the success of their team. It is here where we begin to understand the value and importance of contributing to the success of others and find ways to help out the people around them. In fact, one of my daily goals is to create confidence, clarity, and commitment among my team. This is the solid transition from ME to WE for an entrepreneurial personality type. We have reached the time in our lives where our success is dependent on leading our team and moving them forward. We realize we cannot do it all by ourselves, and in fact, if we want to reach the destination we have in mind, we are going to need more and more help over time.

How does my team get further ahead?

The call of contribution becomes stronger as we look to impart our learnings to our teams in hopes that they will carry on our message. In this stage, the entrepreneurial personality type realizes that leverage for their team is the true path to ultimate success and contribution. Life accomplishments are no longer about what you can do on your own, but instead what you can do through your team and the profound realization that helping them is helping yourself. Here the primary mode of success is building up the people around you.

How do we help others get ahead?

Now it is no longer enough to help those around you. Your mission is bigger than your team, and there are others who can benefit. Entrepreneurs throughout history have transitioned from building their own businesses and contribution to helping others do the same. "How do we help others get ahead?" is one of the foundational questions of our lives, because as evolutionary Hunters, we are driven to help the tribe survive and become better.

How do we help everyone?

The world is made up of people just like you, with needs that you and your teams can address. By living in full contribution, you have the opportunity to reshape our entire world. Throughout the major cities of the world are buildings with the names of famous entrepreneurs from the past. These buildings were erected not just because these individuals were successful, but because they made a massive contribution and most likely paid for them. Entrepreneurs are the small group of people who want to do everything they can to be successful, and then just as fast as they experience success, they give it all away.

Understanding these questions, and seeking out their answers, helps EPTs successfully manage their lives and the people around them. In this way, they are able to fully mobilize themselves and others and significantly contribute to the world.

Some successful EPTs skipped steps but then came back to them later in their careers. Others repeated steps over and over again until they learned to move toward living in full contribution.

More than just outlining the structure behind the lives of successful EPTs, these questions illuminate a key truth that I hope you have noticed throughout this book. It is simple but profound. It is spoken often yet is not always heard. It is the driving force behind my desire to discover and educate the world about the Entrepreneurial Personality Type.

It is this one fact...

You are not alone.

Conclusion

Dear EPT,

You're here reading this right now because deep down you've always known the truth. You're different. The way you think, the way you dream, and the way you process the world around you sets you apart. You can't help but stand out, even when you try to stick to the shadows.

It's time to stop hiding in the shadows. There's nothing wrong with you and you are not alone. In fact, we desperately need your endless drive and your burning desire to make the world a better place. You are part of a tribe of empire builders, game changers, and trailblazers. You are who I wrote this book for, and here is what I want for you.

When most of the population desperately clings to the status quo…move.

When the majority clings to tradition and fights change...innovate.

When the opposition tries to silence you and keep you small...grow.

The truth is, you terrify the rest of the world because they don't know what to do with someone who doesn't fit into their box. But guess what? You're not the only one living outside the box. We are out here...people just like you, your tribe.

You are not alone. I've written this book to help you understand yourself better so you can crush limiting beliefs and start generating the kind of forward progress only EPTs are capable of.

So here's to being different, standing out, pressing forward, and making your greatest contribution.

Here's to your momentum.

Alex Charfen

About the Author

Alex Charfen has dedicated his life to answering the question "How do you make business grow?" which evolved into a larger calling to understand "How do you help people grow?" It was this transition that led him, quite unexpectedly, to uncover a previously mislabeled and misunderstood population among us: the Entrepreneurial Personality Type®(EPT). For the past two decades, Alex has created and curated business philosophies, models, and strategies geared specifically to entrepreneurs. An expert in business growth who has consulted for Fortune 500 and Global 100 companies, Alex is often invited to share his strategies with business owners around the world. He is regularly called upon by major media outlets, including MSNBC, CNBC, FOX News, The Wall Street Journal, USA Today, and The Huffington Post to provide his unique views and insights.

As cofounder and CEO of CHARFEN, Alex helps entrepreneurs and small businesses find momentum to create strong, lasting growth. He lives in Austin, Texas, with his wife, Cadey, and their daughters, Reagan and Kennedy.

Facebook: charfen
Instagram: AlexCharfen
Twitter: @AlexCharfen
YouTube: Charfen
www.billionairecode.com

If You're An Entrepreneurial Personality Type, It's Not a Question Of WHETHER You're On The Path To Entrepreneurial Success...
But WHERE On The Path You Stand Right Now

Throughout history, all the empire builders and game changers—everyone you've ever heard of who has made a massive impact in the world—followed the exact same process on their journey to success. I call this process the Billionaire Code.

The Billionaire Code outlines the different stages of entrepreneurship and exactly what you need to do to ascend from one lever to the next. One of the biggest areas of wasted entrepreneurial potential today is focusing on the right thing but at the wrong time. When you know exactly what you need to do next to move forward, progress becomes infinitely easier.

Complete our short Billionaire Code assessment and we will show you...

- Exactly where you are on the Billionaire Code right now.
- What you should be focused on today to get to the next level.
- The transitions every great entrepreneur faces.
- How to blaze through transitions and stay in momentum.

Don't wait another day to start moving up the Billionaire Code.

Visit www.BillionaireCode.com/EPT today.